What Would YOU Do?

The Salem Witchcraft Trials

Would You Join the Madness?

Elaine Landau

Enslow Elementary
an imprint of
Enslow Publishers, Inc.
40 Industrial Road
Box 398
Berkeley Heights, NJ 07922
USA

http://www.enslow.com

Enslow Elementary, an imprint of Enslow Publishers, Inc.
Enslow Elementary® is a registered trademark of Enslow Publishers, Inc.

Library of Congress Cataloging-in-Publication Data

Landau, Elaine.
The Salem Witchcraft Trials : would you join the madness? / by Elaine Landau.
pages cm. — (What would you do?)
Includes index.
Summary: "Examine the major witchcraft trials in U.S. history. Readers decide what they would do, and then find out what really happened"—Provided by publisher.
ISBN 978-0-7660-4224-7
1. Trials (Witchcraft)—Massachusetts—Salem—Juvenile literature. 2. Witchcraft—Massachusetts—Salem—Juvenile literature. [1. Trials (Witchcraft)—Massachusetts—Salem. 2. Witchcraft—Massachusetts—Salem—History—17th century.] I. Title.
KFM2478.8.W5L35 2014
345.744'50288—dc23
                                2013008787

Future editions:
Paperback ISBN: 978-1-4644-0391-0
EPUB ISBN: 978-1-4645-1215-5
Single-User PDF ISBN: 978-1-4646-1215-2
Multi-User PDF ISBN: 978-0-7660-5847-7

Printed in the United States of America

052014 Lake Book Manufacturing, Inc., Melrose Park, IL

10 9 8 7 6 5 4 3 2 1

To Our Readers: We have done our best to make sure all Internet Addresses in this book were active and appropriate when we went to press. However, the author and the publisher have no control over and assume no liability for the material available on those Internet sites or on other Web sites they may link to. Any comments or suggestions can be sent by e-mail to comments@enslow.com or to the address on the back cover.

♻ Enslow Publishers, Inc., is committed to printing our books on recycled paper. The paper in every book contains 10% to 30% post-consumer waste (PCW). The cover board on the outside of each book contains 100% PCW. Our goal is to do our part to help young people and the environment too!

Photo Credits: ©Clipart.com, p. 36; ©Corel Corporation, p. 4; ©Enslow Publishers, Inc., pp.7, 20; A fanciful representation of Rebecca Nurse's trial from *The Witch of Salem, or Credulity Run Mad* by John R. Musick, p. 24; From *A Popular History of the United States. Vol. 2* by William Cullen Bryant. New York: Charles Scribner's Sons, 1878, p. 457, pp. 8, 19(middle); From "Giles Corey of the Salem Farms" (1868), in *The Complete Poetical Works of Henry Wadsworth Longfellow*, Boston, Houghton, 1902, pp. 1, 11, 23; Library of Congress, pp. 31, 32, 35; Shutterstock.com: ©Flying Macaws p. 19(parrot, left); ©Thinkstock: (Dorling Kindersley RF, p. 14; Kasia Biel/Hemera, p.19 (book, right); Photos.com, pp. 15, 27);Vincent Scesney/©Enslow Publishers, Inc., pp. 42, 43; Willjay, taken by me. Rebecca Nurse House, Danvers, Massachusetts/Wikipedia.com, p. 41.

Cover Illustration: ©Thinkstock: Photos.com

Contents

That Very Cold Winter 5

A Terrible Mistake 10

The Witch Hunt Begins 14

From Bad to Worse 18

The Lies Grow 22

Witches, Witches, Everywhere 26

The World Turned Upside Down 30

The Terrible Trials 34

The Beginning of the End 38

Getting Back to Normal 41

Timeline 45

Words to Know 46

Learn More (Books and Web Sites) 47

Index 48

In this painting, "Pilgrims Going to Church" by George H. Boughton, churchgoers walk to church. They needed weapons for protection against wild animals.

That Very Cold Winter

The Time: **The winter of 1691–1692**

The Place: **Salem Village, in what is now Massachusetts**

It was the coldest winter anyone in Salem Village could remember. Most days it snowed. Some snowdrifts were higher than the houses. The winds were strong and biting. They could knock down a small child. Yet few children went out for long that winter. The weather kept them inside.

Even in good weather, Salem Village was not a fun place for young people. There was not much to do. Salem Village had mostly farms. There was also a Meeting House that served as a church too.

The people of Salem Village were very religious. They were known as Puritans. They lived by the Bible. They believed in hard work and prayer. They were against dancing, card playing, and parties. Salem Villagers thought these things were the work of the devil.

That cold winter the young people of Salem Village were very bored. They mostly stayed at home waiting for spring. But things were a bit more interesting at one house. Surprisingly, it was the home of the Village preacher, Rev. Samuel Parris. The preacher lived with his wife and their nine-year-old daughter, Betty. Betty's eleven-year-old cousin, Abigail, lived with them too. But there was another adult in the household. It was a slave woman named Tituba. Tituba cooked and cleaned. She was often with the girls as well.

Tituba was from Barbados. It is an island south of the United States in the Caribbean Sea. The island was nothing like Salem Village. Many people there believed in magic. At times, they cast spells.

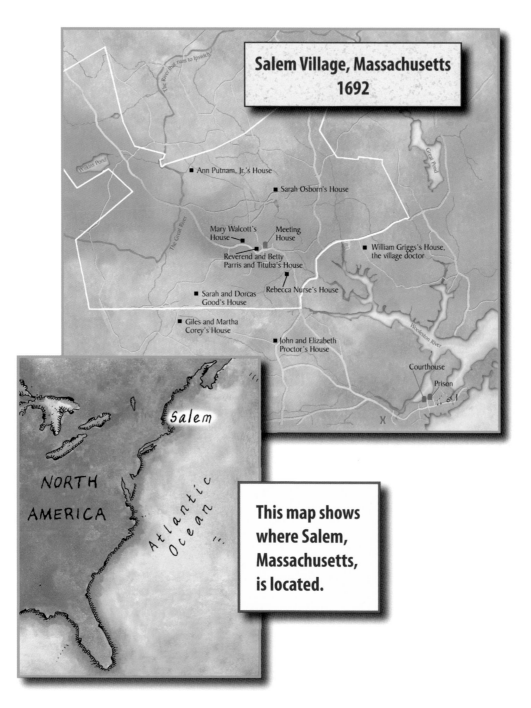

Salem Village, Massachusetts 1692

The River that Turns to Ipswich

Wilkins Pond

■ Ann Putnam, Jr.'s House

■ Sarah Osborn's House

The Great River

Mary Walcott's House ■

Meeting House

Reverend and Betty Parris and Tituba's House

■ William Griggs's House, the village doctor

Great Pond

Rebecca Nurse's House

■ Sarah and Dorcas Good's House

■ Giles and Martha Corey's House

■ John and Elizabeth Proctor's House

Wooleston River

Courthouse

Prison

Salem

NORTH AMERICA

Atlantic Ocean

This map shows where Salem, Massachusetts, is located.

7

Tituba, a slave belonging to Samuel Parris, was at the center of the witch frenzy.

They also played fortune-telling games. Such things would never be allowed in Salem Village. Magic, spells, and fortune-telling were thought to be witchcraft. Witchcraft was both a sin and a crime in Salem Village.

Tituba knew how to cast all kinds of spells. She would also make magic potions. Betty and Abigail loved to hear her stories. So did some of the other young girls in Salem Village. That winter they often visited Betty and Abigail. One of these girls was twelve-year-old Ann Putnam. Some older girls visited too. Among these were sixteen-year-old Mary

Wolcott and seventeen-year-old Elizabeth Hubbard. The oldest was nineteen-year-old Mercy Lewis.

The girls liked Tituba. They begged her to teach them how to tell fortunes. But if Tituba agreed, this would have to be done in secret. If Tituba were found out, she could go to prison or even be hanged.

What Would YOU Do?

What would you do if you were Tituba?

❈ Would you say no to the girls? Was it just too dangerous to do magic in Salem Village? Could Tituba be thought of as a witch? *OR . . .*

❈ Would you give in to the girls? Would you make them promise not to tell anyone? But can a nine-year-old and her friends be trusted to keep such a dangerous secret?

What Really Happened . . .

A Terrible Mistake

Tituba gave in to the girls. She told them stories about black magic. She showed them how to cast spells. She said she could see the future in different shapes. The young girls were thrilled. At first, nothing bad happened. But before long, the trouble began.

In January 1692, Betty started acting strangely. Some days she refused to eat. Other times, she'd start crying for no reason. She often also became very forgetful.

By mid-February Betty's cousin, Abigail, wasn't better. Her behavior frightened people in Salem Village. Without warning, she'd fall to the floor.

Tituba performed acts of sorcery for Betty Parris, Abigail Williams, and other children in the kitchen of the Parris house.

Lying there, her whole body would shake. Now she often made little sense when she spoke. No one understood much of what she said.

Dr. William Griggs was Salem Village's doctor. He examined the girls. But he couldn't find anything physically wrong with them. He decided that they must be bewitched. He didn't know what else could be causing this.

That frightened people in Salem Village. Was there a witch among them? The Villagers hoped not. But the girls did not get any better. Instead, things got worse.

The problem spread. Betty's and Abigail's friends started to act strangely too. Before long, Ann Putnam, Elizabeth Hubbard, Mercy Lewis, Mary Wolcott, and others began acting odd. They'd thrash about on the floor. Sometimes, they would shriek and point to something that wasn't there. Often they seemed to slip into a trance. They'd also hide in a corner and cover their heads. They seemed to want to protect themselves from some terrible unseen demon.

The important men in the Village wanted to know the truth. They were worried about the girls. So they questioned them almost daily. The men demanded that the girls tell who bewitched them.

What Would YOU Do?

What if you were an official in Salem Village?

❊ Would you take this case very seriously? Would you bring charges against anyone the girls said bewitched them? Would these people be tried in court? *OR ...*

❊ Would you see things more calmly? You know the girls were very bored that winter. Could they be pretending now? Maybe these girls just want attention. Should you take their actions seriously?

The Witch Hunt Begins

At first, Betty would not give any names. Then she finally said that Tituba was a witch. Tituba was easy to blame. As a slave, she had no rights.

But the girls did not stop there. They began to name others too. They named women who had never done magic. Yet the girls got away with it. These women were old and poor.

> Had the girls only accused some of the poor old women of Salem Village of being witches?

Two afflicted girls, two women they accused, and the judges who conducted the trials can be seen in this illustration.

They were not well liked and had few friends. If they were accused of being witches, no one would defend them.

One of the women was Sarah Osborne. She had been sick and could not come to church often. Many people saw her as a sinner because of this. Another accused woman was Sarah Good. Sarah was poor and homeless. Sometimes, she didn't make much sense when she spoke.

What Would YOU Do?

What would you do if you were an official in Salem Village?

❀ Would you have the women arrested right away? If they really were witches should they be able to go about freely? After all, you must keep the Villagers safe. *OR* . . .

❀ Would you think carefully before acting? You might wonder why the girls only picked out poor women without families to help them. Would you feel that more than a young girl's word is needed in such cases? Would you demand other proof as well?

From Bad to Worse

Things did not go well for the accused women. Sarah Osborne, Sarah Good, and Tituba were arrested on February 29, 1692. They were questioned at the Meeting House on March 1. The bewitched girls were there too. Lots of people from the Village came as well. They wanted to see the witches. They were also curious about the bewitched girls.

Sarah Osborne and Sarah Good swore they were innocent. Yet as they spoke, the girls hollered, hooted, and made other strange noises. Several of the girls rolled their eyes. Some flung their arms about. It was quite a scene.

Tituba said that the devil had a brightly colored bird perched on his shoulder and had given her a book to sign.

The slave woman, Tituba, said she was a witch. She swore that the devil had come to her wearing a dark suit. He carried a brightly colored bird. He also made her sign a book. She said he forced her to bewitch the girls.

But even that was not enough. The men who were questioning her wanted more. They wanted Tituba to say that the other women were witches too.

The Salem Village officials wanted to know if the girls were pretending or actually under the spell of witches.

What Would YOU Do?

What would you do if you were Tituba?

❀ Would you feel you had no right to say anything about the other women? You could swear that you never did magic with them. That would be the truth. *OR...*

❀ Would you do all you could to save yourself? Would you lie? Would you say that the other women signed the devil's book too? Maybe you think that Reverend Parris will not beat you then. You might even think that later on the court will go easier on you if you say this.

The Lies Grow

Tituba tried to save herself. She said the other women were witches too. In February 1692, all three women were taken to a jail in Boston. They'd stay there until their trials.

Meanwhile the girls accused other people of witchcraft as well. But this time some good church-going women were among them. On March 11, Ann Putnam said that Martha Corey was a witch. Corey rarely missed church. She didn't seem like a witch either. She led a pure and godly life. But when she was questioned on March 21, the girls really acted up. They twisted their bodies into strange shapes. They also copied every move Martha Corey made.

Martha, unlike some of the women first accused, was a respected churchgoer. She repeatedly denied being a witch.

If she nodded her head, they nodded their heads. If she shifted her feet, they did the same.

Soon the girls even accused seventy-one-year-old Rebecca Nurse of being a witch. Nurse was very religious and knew the Bible well. She was kind

Rebecca Nurse's devout manner impressed the jury, which at first declared her not guilty.

and always prayed for those in need. The people of Salem Village loved and respected her.

But by now, the young girls had become fearless. They did not care who they accused. Everyone seemed to believe them. So they felt very powerful.

What Would YOU Do?

What would you do if you were a friend of Rebecca Nurse?

✿ Would you speak up for her? Would you insist that Nurse couldn't possibly be a witch? Would you say that she was just too godly to have a pact with the devil? *OR . . .*

✿ Would you think twice about speaking out? What if you were wrong? What if Nurse wasn't innocent? Would you be helping the devil do his work in Salem Village?

Witches, Witches, Everywhere

A few people in Salem Village stood up for Rebecca Nurse. They said that she loved God. But it was useless. The bewitched girls had pointed her out. Now just about everyone thought she was a witch.

By the end of March, five people had been accused of witchcraft. One was a five-year-old girl named Dorcas. No one knows why she admitted to being a witch. But her mother had been jailed for witchcraft. Maybe the child just wanted to be with her.

Soon enough, people were being accused of witchcraft all over Salem.

Dozens of suspected witches awaited trial inside Salem's Old Witch Jail. This is a recreation of what the cell might have looked like.

What Would YOU Do?

What would you do if you lived in Salem Village and saw this happening?

❋ Would you argue that these women have been unjustly called witches? *OR...*

❋ Would you be too scared to say anything? If you spoke up, you might be called a witch or a wizard (a male witch) next. Then you would have to stand trial as well.

The World Turned Upside Down

At times, people in Salem Village doubted the bewitched girls' claims. John Proctor, a local tavern owner, said that the girls should be whipped. Then on March 28, his wife was accused of being a witch. Soon the girls also said that John Proctor was a wizard. The couple was questioned and jailed with the others in Boston.

Once the trials started, some people thought that the judges were not very fair either. They accepted spectral evidence. This was the belief that a person's spirit can leave his or her body for a while. During that time, the spirit can harm others. The problem was that only the bewitched girls could see these spirits. There could be no other witnesses. So how could those accused defend themselves? They couldn't prove that an unseen spirit hadn't left their bodies.

Who or what were the judges suppose to believe?

This drawing shows the power that many Puritans thought witches had.

What Would YOU Do?

What would you do if you were one of the nine judges hearing the witchcraft cases?

❀ Would you demand that there be more proof than just spectral evidence? *OR* . . .

❀ Would you go along with the other judges? Not all the judges there had solid legal training. But in Salem Village, the law was based on the Bible. So spectral evidence was easily accepted.

The Terrible Trials

By mid-June the witchcraft trials began. There were over 150 people waiting to be tried. Yet four of those never made it to court. They died in jail.

The trials were poorly run. In court, the young girls screamed, twisted their bodies, and fell to the floor. The judges never tried to quiet the girls. They did not even scold them.

Sarah Good was found guilty. She had tried to kill herself three times while still in jail. Then on July 19, she, Rebecca Nurse, and three others were hanged.

The hangings kept on. The bodies were thrown into a large common grave. One man was hanged in his best suit. But thieves took it off his lifeless body.

At times, the hangings worried some people. One minister, Reverend George Burroughs, had been found guilty. Then he recited the Lord's Prayer just before the noose was put around his neck. Puritans believed that a wizard would not be able to do that. It did not matter, though. The man was hanged anyway.

By September 22, twenty people had been hanged. Salem Villagers were getting tired of all the pain and death. The bewitched girls kept on accusing people. They even said some of the judges' relatives were witches.

Governor Phips

By September 29, the Massachusetts Colony Governor William Phips returned from a long trip. He did not like what was happening in Salem Village. The hangings had turned too many young children into orphans. The trials had taken up lots of time too. The Village's farms and businesses were doing poorly. People were too busy going to the trials and hangings.

George Burroughs, the former minister in Salem Village, was hanged despite his ability to say the Lord's Prayer without one mistake.

What Would YOU Do?

What would you do if you were the Governor?

❀ Would you have the courage to do the right thing? Would you call off the arrests and trials? *OR . . .*

❀ Would you let the hangings go on? There were over 100 people in jail. The bewitched girls were still accusing people. Would you dare defy them?

The Beginning of the End

Governor Phips did the right thing. He stood up to the girls. On October 8, the Governor gave an important order. He stopped the witchcraft trials that were underway. Those in jail waiting to be hanged were freed as well.

Not everyone found guilty of witchcraft was hanged. They had a choice. They could be freed if they admitted they were guilty. They also had to promise to give up their evil ways. They were to have nothing more to do with the devil.

Some people who were accused of witchcraft did this. But most refused. Their good name was important to most Puritans. They would not admit to a crime they did not commit. In these cases, it cost them their lives.

That's what happened with seventy-one-year-old Giles Corey. Corey refused to say he was a wizard. His jailors tortured him to make him admit it. They placed heavy stones on the old man's body. The pain was terrible and two days later he died. But he never said he'd worked with the devil.

What Would YOU Do?

What would you do if you were accused of witchcraft in Salem Village?

❊ Would you say you did it to save your life? *OR . . .*

❊ Would you refuse to say you were a witch or wizard? Would you be willing to die for your beliefs and to keep your good name?

This recreation shows what Rebecca Nurse's house looked like at the time of the Salem Witch Trials.

Getting Back to Normal

Most people in Salem Village refused to say they practiced witchcraft. They took pride in living a moral life. That's why so many were hanged.

Historians are people who study history. Over time, many have looked at what happened in Salem Village. Here are just a few reasons the witchcraft trials might have taken place.

The trials might have been partly due to family feuds. The Putnams were an old and powerful family in Salem Village. Young Ann Putnam was one of the girls thought to be bewitched. Many of those she accused were people her parents had disliked and fought with for years.

The Salem Witch Museum has many exhibits that bring you back to 1692 Salem.

Land could have been another reason for some of the hangings. Those guilty of witchcraft lost their land. Some of these farms had good fertile plots. When a witch's land was taken, other Villagers could usually buy it at a very low price. Some people might have wanted this property. It might have stopped them from speaking out at a trial.

GEORGE JACOBS
HANGED
AUGUST 19, 1692

REBECCA NURSE
HANGED
JULY 19, 1692

These stones are part of a wall in Salem. It is a memorial to those people who were executed during the witch trials. Each stone sticking out from the wall has a person's name carved into it.

It's also been thought that the young girls might have had ergot poisoning. Ergot is a type of fungus. It grows on grain which is used to make bread. Grain was grown in and around Salem Village. Ergot poisoning could have caused the girls to act as they did.

But the most likely cause for the behavior of the young girls was probably much simpler. They could have just been bored. Being "bewitched" brought them lots of attention. That winter they were the "rock stars" of Salem Village.

Yet the pain and damage they caused was horrible. The adults around them took them too seriously. Even today, the area is known for those trials.

Salem Village is now what is known as the town of Danvers, Massachusetts. There are lots of witchcraft museums there. You can still see where Rebecca Nurse's farm was. There is even a park built in honor of those who so unfairly died. What happened in Salem Village serves as an important reminder. Laws and courts are needed to keep order. But they are worthless unless they are fair and just.

Timeline

1691–1692—Winter is one of the coldest ever in Salem Village.

1692 *(January)*—Betty Parris starts behaving strangely. She is thought to be bewitched.

(mid-February)—Betty's friends start acting bewitched.

(February 29)—Tituba, Sarah Good, and Sarah Osborne are arrested.

(March 1)—The three women (listed above) are questioned at the Meeting House.

(March 11)—Ann Putnam accuses Martha Corey of witchcraft.

(March 21)—Martha Corey is questioned at the Meeting House.

(March 28)—Elizabeth Proctor is accused of witchcraft.

(April 11)—Elizabeth Proctor's hearing is held. During the hearing, John Proctor is accused of being a wizard.

(July 19)—Five people are hanged.

(August 19)—Five more people are hanged.

(September)—Still more people are executed. In all, 20 people die during the witchcraft trials.

(October 8)—The Governor of the Massachusetts Colony orders that there be no further arrests or trials for witchcraft in Salem Village.

(October 29)—The Governor of the Massachusetts Colony closes the court set up to hear these cases.

1752—Salem Village becomes the town of Danvers, Massachusetts.

Words to Know

antics—Clownish behavior or pranks.

Barbados—An island country in the West Indies.

bewitch—To cast a spell on someone.

black magic—Magic done for an evil purpose.

Caribbean Sea—Part of the Atlantic Ocean between the West Indies and South and Central America.

feud—A long-standing argument between families.

historian—Someone who studies history.

official— Someone who holds an important government position.

spectral evidence—The idea that a person's spirit can leave his or her body and do harm to another person.

spell— Words that are thought to have magical powers.

trance—Being in a daze-like state.

witness—A person who has seen or heard something important.

wizard—A male witch.

Learn More

Books

Becker, Ann. *Wizard, Witches, & Dragons.* Vero Beach, Fla.: Rourke Publishing, 2009.

Fradin, Judith Bloom, and Dennis Brindell Fradin. *The Salem Witch Trials.* Tarrytown, N.Y.: Benchmark Books, 2009.

Kerns, Ann. *Wizards and Witches.* Minneapolis, MN: Lerner Publications, 2009.

Pipe, Jim. *You Wouldn't Want to Be a Salem Witch! Bizarre Accusations You'd Rather Not Face.* Danbury, Conn.: Franklin Watts, 2009.

Stern, Steven L. *Witchcraft in Salem.* New York: Bearport, 2010.

Waxman, Laura Hamilton. *Who Were the Accused Witches of Salem? And Other Questions About the Witchcraft Trials.* Minneapolis, MN: Lerner Publications, 2012.

Web Sites

The Museum of Witchcraft
<http://www.museumofwitchcraft.com>

Salem Witch Museum
<http://www.salemwitchmuseum.com>

Index

B

Barbados, 6–8
Bible, 6, 23, 33
Burroughs, George, 35

C

Corey, Giles, 39
Corey, Martha, 22

E

ergot poisoning, 44

F

family feuds, 41
fortune telling, 6–10

G

Good, Dorcas, 26
Good, Sarah, 16, 18, 34
Griggs, William, 10–12

H

hangings, 34–35, 38
Hubbard, Elizabeth,
    8–9, 12

L

Lewis, Mercy, 9, 12
Lord's Prayer, 35

M

memorials, 43, 44

N

Nurse, Rebecca, 23–26,
    34

O

Osborne, Sarah, 16, 18

P

Parris, Betty, 6, 8, 10
Parris, Samuel, 6
Phips, William, 35, 38
Proctor, John, 30
property confiscation,
    42
Puritans, 6, 35, 38
Putnam, Ann, 8, 12, 41

S

Salem Village, 5–6, 41
spectral evidence,
    30–31, 33

T

theft, 34
Tituba
    accusation of, 14

arrest, trial of, 18–20,
    22
as teacher, 6–10
torture, 39

W

Williams, Abigail, 6, 8,
    10–12
witchcraft, 8
witchcraft museums, 44
witchcraft trials
    accusations, 14–16,
        22–26, 35
    admission of guilt, 39
    ending of, 38–39
    girl's symptoms,
        10–13, 22
    motivations, 6, 25,
        41–44
    opposition to, 30, 35
    proceedings, 18–19,
        22, 30–31, 34
    results of, 35, 44
wizards, 30, 35, 39
Wolcott, Mary, 8–9, 12